Thursday November th 20	Starbut boat Struck A whale and kild
	Larbut boat Struck A whale and kild Lat 33.33 S Long 7...30 East
Friday November th 21 1834	Larbut boat S____ ___ and boat Stever ___ she sunk Lat. 33.41 S Long 07.04.15 East
Saturday November th 22 1835	Struck A whale two the waist boat and parted the Lines and struck one two the larbut boat and drawede and struck one two the starbut boat and drawed all done in 5 minits Lat 34..01 S Long 07..00 East
Thursday November th 27 1834	Larbut boat Struck a whale and kild Lat 33.50 S Long 07.07.00 East

Drawed the irons

Drawed the irons

WHALE SHIPS AND WHALING

THE ENDPAPERS REPRODUCE TWO FACING PAGES FROM
THE LOGBOOK OF THE WHALER ROYAL WILLIAM,
DATED 1834.

WHALE SHIPS
AND WHALING

BY ALBERT COOK CHURCH

BONANZA BOOKS · NEW YORK

CONTENTS

PREFACE

IN preparing this volume it has been my purpose to assemble a more complete descriptive photographic history covering whale ships and whaling than has heretofore existed between the covers of a book.

Born in New Bedford of a family of seafaring people, it has been my good fortune to enjoy a lifetime of close association with whaleships and whalemen. My natural love for ships has grown steadily with the passing years and my interest and pride have increased through part ownership of ten whaling vessels in years gone by.

Among these ships was the *Charles W. Morgan,* and although I was part owner I never saw her until she returned to her home port of New Bedford after twenty years' operation out of San Francisco in the Arctic and Northern Pacific fishery. This grand old ship, now nearly a hundred years old, is still preserved and still with us, having weathered, with only slight damage, the devastating hurricane of September 1938 that roared along the New England coast. Thus it was not only an intimate knowledge of their sturdy build and construction but an ever growing fondness and respect for these wonderful ships which gave inspiration for the purpose of this book.

The pen drawing of the oil cooling tank between decks aboard the old bark *Commodore Morris* I made more than forty years ago when light conditions were not sufficient for a camera study. From that time on, whenever opportunity offered, I proceeded by means of photography to assemble a thorough coverage of whaleships and whaling—from the building of the ship through the various stages of her existence and activity, until battered and worn she was cast aside to be broken up.

9

The photographs of whaling operations at sea were secured by sending cameras and equipment in care of ship's officers who co-operated by taking pictures when occasion permitted. Those appearing in this book were made either by Captain Henry Mandley, Jr., aboard the schooner *John R. Manta,* or by Captain and Mrs. J. A. M. Earle aboard the *Charles W. Morgan.* Many were lost through atmospheric conditions prevailing in the whaling grounds at sea, but those possible to reconstruct well rewarded the efforts involved.

Many months' work was required to restore some of the old wet plate prints which the passage of time had almost obliterated; and some negatives were actually rebuilt from broken bits of glass. Gathered together in this book the illustrations represent years of patient search and tedious work to achieve a pictorial record of the industry.

By reference to old log books it has been possible to reach back over a period of more than a century and recapture the intimate life and adventures aboard ship when the pursuit and capture of whales was becoming one of the most important industries in our early national existence.

The model builder will find authentic data in the detail photographs of the *Charles W. Morgan,* taken with but few exceptions while she was still in active service. The lines of the *Contest,* taken from the builder's half-model, along with spar and sail plans are reproduced from original material in my possession.

It is my hope that these few remarks combined with the historical background and descriptive text which follow will contribute to the reader's enjoyment and a more thorough understanding of the illustrations.

I gratefully acknowledge the assistance of Mr. Howard I. Chapelle and Mr. Robert E. Farlow in the preparation of this book, and I hope it will prove of permanent interest and value to those who follow the sea in ships and books.

Albert Cook Church

FAIRHAVEN, MASS.

Part One

WHALESHIPS
AND WHALING

1. CHIEFLY HISTORICAL
A Brief Sketch of the Whale Fishery

THOUGH the Yankee whaleship has disappeared from the seas, and the picturesque industry is a thing of the past, the story of the origin, rise and decline of the whale fishery presents much of historical interest, and few industries have a more remarkable history.

Primarily these monsters of the deep were chiefly prized as food; the later discovery of their commercial value and importance led to the gradual development of a definite industry. The Biscayans claimed to be the first actually to hunt whales, while others claim the Norwegians were the pioneers. Whale fishing is mentioned along the French coast as early as the year 875, but whether this referred to cutting up stranded whales or an established fishery is uncertain. Up to the sixteenth century the Norwegians, French, Icelanders and English had been engaged in the fishery, but to what extent is not known. However, most authorities give the Biscayans credit for being first to capture whales, and agree the date was about 1575.

By 1620 the fishery had reached such development by the English and Dutch at Spitzbergen that the New England colonists were undoubtedly familiar with its methods and products, for Captain John Smith turned aside from the object of his voyage to pursue whales which were so plentiful along the New England coast.

The history of the American whale fishery may thus be said to begin with that of the colonies themselves, although several decades elapsed before it became firmly established. Quite likely the native Indians were skilled in capturing whales long before this date, for we find mention in the early colonial records of whale meat used as food, and reference by a Plymouth historian to the boldness shown by Indians who attacked these huge monsters from open canoes, killing them by crude spears attached to logs by twisted vines.

Finding the soil unproductive and difficult to cultivate, the colonists turned toward the sea as a dependable source of food supply, as both whales and fish were abundant. During the warmer season whales swarmed around the shores, and many were captured when stranded on the sand bars along the coast. With an eye to the importance of the whale fishery, Massachusetts passed an Act in 1639 to encourage it, providing that vessels engaged in whaling were tax exempt for a period of seven years, and those employed were excused from military service during the whaling season.

The earliest organized American whale fishery was conducted along the shores of Long Island, where the town of Southampton, settled in 1640 by an offshoot from the Massachusetts colony of Lynn, was divided into four wards of eleven persons each, taking turns to cut up drift whales cast ashore. The whales were cut up, blubber tried out, and the profits shared by "Every inhabitant with his child or servant that is above sixteen years of age," those performing the labor receiving an extra share.

Whaling soon assumed the proportions of a permanent enterprise, and in 1672 we find the inhabitants of Nantucket busily engaged in carrying on the industry from shore. Tall spars were erected on the beach on which lookouts were stationed, and when whales were sighted offshore the alarm was given and the whales pursued in small boats kept ready for the occasion. The natives fashioned crude harpoon irons with which to capture them, towing them ashore to remove the blubber. The services of experienced Cape Cod whalemen were secured to teach the best methods of killing whales and boiling out the oil, and Nantucket whalemen became so expert they were famous the world over. Plenty of whales were close at hand, and no difficulty was experienced in producing all the oil required.

Sloops fitted for cruises of a few weeks came into use, carrying enough casks to contain the blubber of one whale. Sailing usually in pairs, they divided their catch equally while in company, sometimes becoming separated by stormy weather. They usually carried two boats, one held in reserve in case the one lowered for whales became damaged.

When a cargo was secured, they returned home and were beached broadside to shore. The butts containing blubber were hoisted out and drawn by ox teams to tryworks built on the beach close at hand, where the blubber was cut up, sliced, and tried out. Shore tryworks were in use many years after exclusive shore whaling ceased, for as whales became wary of coastal waters and passed farther off to the banks, they were followed by larger and more seaworthy sloops built for this purpose. Until 1715 sloops of twelve to thirty tons were used in the fishery, and among them the *Hope* of forty tons was considered a very giant. The log book of sloop *Betsy* states that "Tryworks were knocked down" when returning from a voyage in 1762, indicating that trying out was then done on board, making longer and more profitable voyages possible. At that time it was the custom to haul vessels on shore during the severe winter weather, to escape damage by drift and pack ice floes.

As whales grew scarce in the vicinity of shore, cruises extended from adjacent waters and the banks to the Virginia capes. Sloops for this fishery were of sixty to seventy tons, carrying about fourteen men in the crew. Soon larger sloops, schooners and brigs were built as cruises gradually lengthened, by 1770 extending to the waters off Brazil, Guiana and the Western Islands, while Davis Strait had been reached in 1732.

The Revolutionary War dealt a terrific blow to the American fishery

15

at this period. British frigates seized American whaleships wherever found and forced their hardy crews into the King's service. They were given their choice of manning British men-of-war or whaling vessels, the British endeavoring to grasp the fishery from the American colonies by this means.

Nantucket suffered the loss of 134 whaleships, her fleet numbering 150 before the war. Although demoralized, the fishery revived rapidly at the close of the war in 1783, in spite of the fact that England and France made strenuous efforts to transplant the industry to their own shores. Massachusetts offered a bounty, and England and France with greater wealth held out strong inducements, finally inducing a number of whalemen to form a colony near Halifax, Nova Scotia, in 1786. They built wharves, warehouses, sperm candle factories, etc.; but although fairly prosperous for a while, they became dissatisfied, some returning to Nantucket, while others went to England and settled at Milford Haven.

The dawn of peace and independence brought increasing ambition among American whaleship merchants, and no longer harassed upon the high seas they fitted ships for longer and more extensive voyages. By 1789 they reached Madagascar and soon passed into the southern Pacific, where their pluck and enterprise were abundantly rewarded, for they returned deeply laden with rich cargoes of oil and bone, whales being found in countless numbers.

Whaleships of the eighteenth century were hardly equal in model or build to the vessels that came afterward when merchants and whalemen had accumulated more wealth and experience. They were short, bluff-bowed craft, averaging 250 tons; slow and unwieldy under most favorable conditions. They were sent to sea uncoppered, and cruised nearly their entire voyages in warm latitudes where marine growth and barnacles form quickly on uncoppered hulls, an easy prey to teredo worms. The wonder is that these clumsy old craft ever managed to drift back to Nantucket.

It was customary to call at the convenient islands in the Pacific to overhaul hull and gear, replenish stores with vegetables and tropical fruits, and ship home from foreign ports oil and whalebone taken on the outward cruise to enable them to carry more on the return voyage. Larger ships were built and coppered. New Bedford soon took the lead, outstripping Nantucket both in number of vessels and tonnage. The shoal waters about the harbor entrance at Nantucket made it nearly impossible for ships of heavy tonnage to enter without lightering cargo, if deeply laden, and floating pontoons called "camels" were built to overcome this inconvenience. Doubtless these handicaps were at least partially responsible for the fact that most of the large type whaleships built after this period hailed from mainland ports.

The War of 1812 and the British practice of impressing crews of American ships created serious damage to the whaling industry, and many whalers fell prey to British privateers before they had heard of the war. This wholesale destruction by the British proved their undoing, however, for upon learning they were seizing American whaleships in the South Pacific, the U.S. frigate *Essex* recaptured the prizes and destroyed whaleships of the enemy. The *Essex* practically swept British whaleships from the seas, and their Pacific fishery never recovered.

After the treaty was signed in 1814 the impressment ceased, and whaling began to pick up lost ground. The three decades following 1820 were the golden age of American whalemen. Voyages were carried to greater extremes and became correspondingly more profitable. Three- and four-year voyages were the rule, and even longer in many instances.

New grounds were located where whales seemed to exist in unlimited number, and in 1835 the ship *Ganges* of Nantucket opened the northwest coast right whale fishery. Pushing farther into the frozen north, the ships *Hercules* and *Janus* of New Bedford captured the first bowhead whales off the coast of Kamchatka in 1843, and five years later the

Sag Harbor bark *Superior* sailed through Bering Strait to attack the bowheads in the Arctic.

The fishery reached its highest development and prosperity about 1857, the New Bedford fleet numbering 329 whaleships at that time. But with the Civil War came new disasters that doomed the fishery.

The Confederate cruiser *Shenandoah* caught the Arctic whaling fleet unawares in 1865, captured and burned twenty-five ships—mostly large ones—and bonded four others. Rebel cruisers destroyed fifty whaleships, of which twenty-eight were owned in New Bedford. Many whalers were sold and others transferred to the merchant service. The United States government purchased forty to furnish the larger portion of the so-called "Stone fleet," sunk off Savannah and Charleston harbors to prevent entrance of blockade runners, and this shipping was seldom replaced save by building an occasional vessel.

Following, but six years later, in September 1871, thirty-three whaleships were abandoned in the Arctic, hopelessly crushed in the ice; in 1876 twelve more were lost in a similar manner. Again, in August 1888, five whaleships were lost, this time by a terrific gale off Point Barrow in the Arctic Ocean. Scarcely a season went by without several such disasters, although these were the most notable. Many a staunch ship left her bones to bleach on some distant shore, while the perilous ice fields, sunken coral reefs and tropical hurricanes claimed occasional victims from the steadily diminishing fleet.

Although the fishery made a feeble effort to regain its prestige, the discovery of mineral oil and the relative cheapness of petroleum further reduced the demand for sperm and whale oil to such a degree that there was no longer any profit in conducting that part of the industry, and ships were constantly withdrawn from service and dismantled in port upon completion of their voyages. About 1880, most of the larger vessels, fitted with steam as auxiliary power, engaged in the Arctic fishery where the heavy catches of whalebone were still a source of profit. The steam whalers, as they were called, were handier to navigate among the ice pack than the exclusively sail-propelled craft, and for several years proved very successful. They made voyages during the season when the ice pack separated, sometimes wintering in the Arctic, but otherwise returning to San Francisco, where they refitted.

The last sailing whaleship abandoned the Arctic fishery years ago, and one by one the small fleet of steam whalers disappeared. Some were lost battling the treacherous ice floes that hemmed them in on all sides; others limped slowly back to San Francisco and were condemned as unfit for further service. The surviving few ships hailing from New Bedford, that for twenty years or more had been in the Arctic fishery, turned their prows homeward, around the Horn, and after a brief pause in port were again returned to sperm whaling in the Atlantic.

The most famous of the remaining fleet was the splendid old whale-ship *Charles W. Morgan,* built at New Bedford in 1841, and named after one of the most successful and representative whaling merchants of his time. This grand old ship, ninety-seven years old and still in existence today as these lines are written, has a most remarkable record.

During the eighty years the *Morgan* was in active service as a whaler she made thirty-seven voyages, cruising in the Arctic and Antarctic, the Atlantic and Pacific, Japan and Okhotsk Seas, and the Indian Ocean. Her trail covered every known sea where whales were found, and her log books reveal that she covered more miles and took more whales than any other whaleship.

The log books also show the *Morgan* had her share of the trials and tribulations apt to occur to any vessel engaged in the whale fishery. She had been ashore, had a few mutinies at sea, and was set on fire once by the crew. She weathered two hurricanes and was struck by lightning three times. A blazing passenger steamer drifted across New Bedford harbor while the *Morgan* was in port and sank alongside, a flaming torch; but the *Morgan* escaped with no further damage than blistered paint on a few of her scorched oaken planks.

On her final whaling voyage, September 9, 1920, the *Charles W. Morgan* sailed from New Bedford, returning to port the following year, May 28, 1921, with a catch of seven hundred barrels of sperm oil.

Originally rigged as a ship, the *Morgan* was known as a single topsail full-rigged whaleship until 1876, when she was altered into a bark rig with double topsails. During 1925 she was again rigged as a ship and placed in a sand berth at South Dartmouth, Massachusetts. In 1941 she was moved to the Marine Historical Association at Mystic, Connecticut, where she is now permanently berthed. Everything practical has been done to preserve this wonderful old whaleship.

While the *Morgan* remains an outstanding example of her type, it was by no means uncommon for whaleships to reach a ripe old age during service: in fact the bark *Rousseau* was in commission eighty-seven years, and the ship *Maria* was broken up in 1872 after being in service ninety years. Bark *Canton* was lost in her seventy-sixth year off the Azores, and when fitting for that voyage on the railway her keel was found to be straight as a gunbarrel.

No wonder they reached such a ripe old age, for better ships were never built. Live oak and copper fastened. Before leaving port they were repaired from keel to truck to withstand the terrific strains to which a whaleship was subjected. Not only did they have to contend with severe storms and hurricanes at sea, with no possible hope for shelter, as did other deep-water ships, but there were the unusual strains of cutting-in huge whales alongside, wrenching at their fluke chains in plunging seas. Master shipwrights, and riggers who wove the intricate maze of hemp and manila from deadeye to to'gallant truck, all took pride in the calling they knew so well, and did the best they knew.

The American whale fishery has passed into history. The *Morgan* alone remains, a monument to the industry and the American whalemen that brought its fame.

20

2. ABOUT WHALESHIPS
AND WHALING

WHALESHIPS differed materially from any other type of merchant ship or clipper in model and equipment, and in fact both sides of a whaleship differed from each other above the waterline.

Speed was the most important essential for the tea clippers, it being necessary to return from China to New York as quickly as possible to prevent deterioration of their cargo and secure top prices for earliest arrival. Whaleships, on the other hand, carried a large amount of special gear and equipment not required by clippers and other merchant ships, such as heavy brick tryworks, iron trypots, cooling tanks, casks for oil, whalecraft and gear for capturing, cutting-in and trying out whale blubber, spare whaleboats, etc., as well as general supplies for voyages covering a period of from three to five years.

Whalers, which averaged between 250 and 400 tons, and but little more than 100 feet in length on deck, necessarily were more bulky in model than ships built expressly for speed. The ratio of beam to length of clipper ships averaged one to six, whereas it was approximately one to four in whaleships. Seaworthiness and ability to carry a full cargo of oil together with the mass of whaling gear and food supplies were the prime consideration in planning whalers, yet many of them were beautifully modeled, and the lines of the ship *Contest* taken off the original builder's model are worthy of close study.

Above the waterline whaleships differed greatly from any other type of merchant vessel, for on the port side three whaleboats were usually carried slung from wooden davits about ten feet in height, while another was carried at the starboard quarter, and most of the larger ships also carried a starboard bow boat. The space amidships abreast the main hatch on the starboard side was reserved for a removable section of the bulwarks called the gangway, which was removed when cutting-in whales to facilitate handling the heavy blanket pieces of blubber.

The tryworks, erected on deck forward of the fore hatch, consisted of a brick furnace containing two iron trypots, each having a capacity of about 250 gallons. Around the base was a low wooden framework, perhaps a foot in height, called the "goose pen," kept filled with sea water. The ground tier of brickwork supporting the trypots was laid checkerboard fashion in such manner that the water flowed freely beneath to prevent the ship taking fire.

A copper tank for cooling hot oil and usually a spare trypot were secured at either side of the tryworks, and a cooper's bench behind it, between the furnace and the hatch. Two small deckhouses were built at the stern at either side of the steering wheel, connected overhead to form a shelter for the helmsman. This was usually referred to as the hurricane house. The cook's galley occupied the house at the starboard side, the other being used as handy lockers for cooperage tools, supplies, etc., and the entrance to the stairway that led to the captain's quarters and cabin below. Directly forward of the traveling steering wheel was a large skylight that gave ample light to the main cabin beneath, and a few feet farther forward was a well-ventilated pen built of slatwork used for potatoes and other vegetables, important items of the food supply.

Aboard the square-rigged whaleships an overhead shelter was also built over the tryworks to shield them in stormy weather, and another between the main and mizzenmasts to accommodate two or three extra whaleboats in case those in use became too badly stove for repair on shipboard.

Aloft, the whaleship differed little from other merchant ships, save for the masthead hoops for lookouts watching for whales on the grounds. They were the most strongly built ships afloat, rigged to withstand unusual strains which wrench their hulls beyond the ability of merchant ships to withstand. A strong statement, perhaps, but their record proves it true.

3. FITTING FOR SEA

FITTING a whaleship for sea was indeed a complicated proceeding, including as it did the workmanship of many skilled tradesmen and mechanics, and the systematic assembly of hundreds of items required for whaling at sea and maintenance of the ship.

Before ship railways were common it was the custom to "heave down" vessels for repairing, caulking and coppering the bottom. This was accomplished by reaving a heavy chain strap around the mainmast head above the maintop truck to which the heaving blocks and tackle were attached. The heaving gear consisted of a pair of huge blocks of tremendous strength, the lower one securely fastened to a large post deeply buried in the wharf a few yards away from the caplog, commonly called the heaving post. The upper block was hooked into the chain strap at the masthead, and the cable rove through the blocks, which had three or four sheaves, leading from the upper block finally to a single sheave tail block secured just inside the heaving post, thence to the revolving winch which took up the cable as the ship gradually hove down on her side. The winch was somewhat like a regular ship's capstan, and four ship carpenters could heave down a large whaleship with comparative ease.

To take the strain off the mainmast head and main rigging another heavy chain led from a fastening beneath the main chain plates, over a block of timber sufficiently thick to clear the bulwarks, to the mast-

24

head. This chain carried the principal strain and relieved the main rigging. Ships were hove down by this means until the keel was above water, enabling the caulkers to caulk the seams thoroughly, after which the bottom was given a coating of boiling hot pitch, then a layer of inch-thick pine sheathing, and finally the outer protective sheathing of copper or yellow metal.

As work proceeded, the position of the ship was regulated by slacking away the falls until the ship was again on an even keel, when the craft was turned around to repair the opposite side. Heaving down was practiced for many years, until the later introduction of ship railways when it was abandoned.

When ship carpenters and caulkers have completed repairs and the ship is again floating on an even keel, recoppered and thoroughly sound below the waterline, the gang of riggers are ready to proceed. In fact, they have been hard at work in the rigging loft while the shipwrights were repairing the hull. Under the watchful eye of a master rigger the great hemp shrouds have been stretched taut as bowstrings, served and tarred with Stockholm tar, and laid aside. These will replace those that became chafed or worn during previous voyages, and are piled on rugged trucks together with a veritable maze of rigging, coils of Russian hemp, marlin and tackle blocks of all sizes.

The riggers swarm over the ship from stem to stern, alow and aloft, swinging about the rigging nimbly as monkeys as they hoist and set the topmasts and topgallant masts in place, sling the yards and reave the running rigging. Once in position, topmasts and topgallant masts are scraped down and oiled; the trucks, lower masts and yards are always painted white.

Painters are busily at work below decks slicking up the cabin and officers' quarters; the deck structures gleam in coats of white; and here and there about the waterways and bits of molding may be seen a touch of blue to delight the sailor's eye. In the old days the black topsides of the hull were varied by a belt of white from stem to stern, with usually nine black painted ports equally spaced, a custom which originated during the days of pirates and enemy ships, which could not determine at great distance whether the vessel were a whaleship or man-of-war.

The wharves are covered with barrels, boxes, cordwood, heaps of heavy chain, and an assortment of whalecraft, including harpoons, lances, cutting spades, oil ladles or bailers, skimmers, grindstones and what not. Drays come lumbering down the dock and unload great folds of canvas, soon to be sent aloft and bent on the tapering yards. The riggers reave on sheets and bend, splice, serve, tar and slush the cordage until the ship fairly glistens in the sun, playing in and out among the folds of canvas as one by one the topsails are shaken out and shimmer in the breeze.

Blocks creak as the heavy casks are lowered into the hold. Barrels of beef, pork, hardbread, flour and numerous food supplies, and casks for water, are stowed below. Other casks of tremendous size contain staves and heads for oil barrels to be assembled by the cooper as required during the voyage, and some may contain supplies of clothing, ship stores, iron hoops, tinware and crockery. Everything likely to be needed during the four-year voyage must be foreseen and provided for in case of emergency, and stowed so the ship will be trimmed properly and the articles found when required.

The ship's carpenter and cooper are busy men indeed; their bench and tools are in order and handy. Potatoes and vegetables are stowed in the pen and the cook straightens things out in the galley. Salt beef is in the harness cask to freshen. The scene of confusion on deck takes on the appearance of order as one by one the articles are placed in proper location. The splendid ship is nearly ready for sea, as well fitted out as riggers, carpenters, painters and caulkers can make her. The captain and officers bring their equipment aboard and arrange their quarters to suit themselves. Compasses are swung in the gimbals, on deck ropes hang in wreathlike coils along the bulwark and flags are flying at the mast-heads, for this is the last Sunday in port.

In another day or two, during which the first of the crew arrive, the ship leaves the wharf alongside a harbor tug and is anchored in mid-stream, there to await the remainder of the crew and date of sailing. Meanwhile the whaleboats are hoisted on the davits and the ship made ready to leave at short notice. The crew continue to arrive in small boats, a few at a time, luggage and all, and disappear down the forecastle companionway.

Down below, forward, the forecastle is a scene of confusion; the babel of foreign tongues mingled with scraping of fiddles, guitars and groaning of accordions; the floor heaped with brightly painted sea chests, bundles and clothes bags.

In the ship's cabin aft, however, everything is in order. Dishes are neatly stowed in the racks, the telltale compass poised in the skylight, barometer and hanging lamps in place, and the ship's clock strikes the hours, adding a homelike cheerfulness to its cozy surroundings.

The remaining stragglers of the crew rounded up, reeking with the familiar odor of rum, the captain boards the ship with his chronometer, and all is ready. The owners and guests assembled to bid the captain good fortune on the voyage will accompany him on the ship for dinner; friends of the crew, less fortunate, are hustled aboard the tug close alongside. The anchor chain is "hove short" and the hawser made fast; the crew break out the anchor and the ship gathers headway, swings slowly around and sweeps proudly seaward, leaving native shores far astern.

Beyond the headlands the more experienced crew go aloft, shake out the topsails one by one, and gradually the ship spreads her wings until everything is set fore and aft, making a beautiful picture as the ship trails along straining at her hawser, seemingly anxious to be away on her voyage.

During the outward passage the captain entertains his friends below, and by the time dinner is over, and perhaps the toast, "a short and greasy voyage," is given to all hands, the ship is well offshore. A sharp blast of the whistle warns the crew to stand by as the tug slackens pace and prepares to take in the hawser. The captain goes forward and gives the word, "Cast off"; overboard goes the hawser, and the ship is on her own.

Guests are hustled into a whaleboat hastily lowered; the yards trimmed aback to check the ship's progress until the boat's return. A few moments more and the boat is again swung from the davits, yards braced around, and the ship is off—perhaps to return a few years later, heavily laden with oil and bone—perhaps to return no more.

4. CRUISING ON THE WHALING GROUNDS

ONCE fairly offshore no time is lost making preparations for the business of the voyage. The captain calls all hands aft, reads the rules governing the ship, explains the objects of the voyage and the necessity for co-operation. Officers and crew receive their instructions, watches and boat crews are chosen, the ship's routine is established and masthead lookouts posted in the "crow's nest" from sunrise to sunset.

Gear for the whaleboats is sorted and placed in position: tub lines stretched and coiled, harpoons and lances ground and sharpened, shafts and sheaths fitted to them and everything made shipshape, ready for whales. Greenhands are taught the ropes and during favorable weather familiarized with whaleboats and gear, and should blackfish be sighted or a school of porpoises they have an opportunity to see them harpooned. Blackfish are a species of small whale, averaging fifteen to twenty feet in length, yielding a fine quality of oil from the head, that from the blubber being of lower grade. Blackfish jaw oil is highly prized for watch, clock and chronometer purposes, and brings a high price to this day.

As the ship nears the whaling grounds the lookouts become more vigilant and scan the horizon eagerly for signs of their quarry. Whales breathe a while on the surface before they sound, or dive below to feed, remaining down practically the same time as a rule: their movements are calculated by timing the intervals. While breathing on the surface they spout frequently, blowing a jet of vapor not unlike steam in ap-

29

pearance that rises to such heights as to be plainly visible for miles in clear weather.

As days pass by the captain paces the deck, anxiously scanning the horizon, until suddenly from aloft comes the cry "Blooows—there she blooows!" Instantly the captain springs into the rigging, fixing his eyes to windward in the direction indicated by the lookout. Sweeping the horizon with his glasses he spies the faint spray of the spouting whale blowing down the wind as he elevates his great flukes and dives to the depths below.

As the whale sounds, the time is carefully noted. Most whalemen allow the whales to sound before launching the boats rather than risk frightening them, for they are wary and become easily alarmed at hearing the boats approach. The line tubs are placed in position and everything made ready to go. At the word to "Lower away," over go the boats and they head to windward in the direction the whale is expected to appear. As they near the locality they spread out to cover a larger area, and eagerly watch for the whale.

The whaleboats are thirty feet in length and six feet wide, each manned by a crew of six, and although slender and shallow carry an incredible amount of gear, the harpoons, lances and tubs of whale line being the most important. Two tubs of line are carried, one containing 225 fathoms and the other 75, used in case the whale sounds to great depth. The line is carefully coiled in the tubs and run aft over the oars around a small post or loggerhead at the stern, leading back over the oars to the bow and made fast to the harpoon, ready for use.

The moment the whale appears the boats head toward the most favorable point of attack, and the harpooner—called the boat steerer, who pulls the bow oar—takes his place by the clumsy cleat at the bow.

The nearest boat creeps stealthily up to the unsuspecting monster, wallowing peacefully on the sea, his first intimation of danger being the sudden plunging of a harpoon deeply into his body. Immediately upon the assurance he is fast, the boat is backed away from danger as the harpooner throws out a few fathoms of slack line and changes ends with the officer, who handles the deadly lance.

The astonished whale, a monster bull, wallows and rolls, beating the sea furiously with his flukes, wondering no doubt what strange calamity has befallen him. Surprise swiftly turns to anger as the harpoon refuses to be dislodged, and elevating his tremendous flukes the stricken whale dives swiftly into the depths of the sea. So great is his speed that the line shrieks and whistles as it burns into the loggerhead and rushes out through the chock at the bow.

The whale's progress is retarded by the turn around the loggerhead and the line allowed to run out as sparingly as the limits of safety permit. An extra turn is taken as his pace slackens, and water is thrown on the line to prevent its taking fire as it roars and groans from the terrific friction. The bow sinks to the water's edge as the extra turn brings up solid—but before the boat is drawn under, the line is slacked away and the whale allowed more freedom.

This is repeated, and more line bent on if necessary, until the whale returns to the surface, when the slack is hastily hauled in and recoiled, enabling them to close in on the whale. Although usually rising some distance away, it occasionally happens that the whale rises directly beneath the boat, crushing it to atoms and either killing or maiming the unfortunate crew.

Whales do not always sound when ironed, sometimes swimming along on the surface at a terrific pace, towing the boat astern in a smother of spray. Old whalemen called this performance the "Nantucket sleigh ride."

As the whale slowly tires from exertion and slackens his speed, the boat is cautiously hauled up alongside, clear of his tremendous flukes. At a favorable opportunity the officer plunges the six-foot steel lance, sharp as a razor, deep into the lungs of the victim, repeating the thrusts with all his strength until the labored spouts become tinged with crimson. The boat must now be hastily worked clear from the thrashing leviathan, swimming and writhing about in a circular course. The death struggle or flurry is near, and death is merely a question of time.

In intense agony the huge cetacean follows its circular course, laboriously thrashing its way through the bloody water, until the throes of death are about to convulse its enormous frame. Great clots of blood, thick as tar, spurt from its spiracle; the sea is lashed furiously into a maelstrom of angry, bloody water—and the ponderous whale after a terrific convulsion rolls slowly over on its side, heading toward the sun, the dorsal fin projecting above water. Whalemen call it "Fin out."

Assuring themselves that the whale is dead by inserting a lance point in the eye, a towline is passed through a hole cut in the head and the whale towed to the ship. Should the ship be close at hand, the towline is passed aboard and the whale hauled alongside.

5. CUTTING-IN THE WHALE

METHODS of cutting-in whales varied somewhat on different ships, the size and species of whale also making a difference in procedure, but the following description may be taken as typical of the general practice among the whaleships engaged in the sperm whale fishery years ago.

The whale, securely moored alongside the ship, must be cut into such sectional strips as may conveniently be taken aboard, a task of no mean proportion. Preparations are made at once for removing and transferring the blubber to the ship. Cutting spades, blubber hooks, mincing knives and incidentals are assembled on deck, the great cutting blocks and tackle sent aloft, and the gangway—a portion of the starboard bulwarks amidship opposite the main hatch—removed for the huge blanket pieces of blubber to swing inboard.

The "cutting stage," a platform upon which the officers stand when cutting the whale's body beneath them, is swung out over the whale. The stage is really a heavy plank extended outward from the side of the ship about ten feet by a plank at each end, making a convenient footing for the men, and an iron railing waist-high enables them to steady themselves and work more freely, for it is a dangerous proceeding in rough weather.

The heavy iron fluke chain is passed around the body near the flukes, one end slipped through a ring at the other end and hove taut by the windlass, forming a slip noose around the whale's flukes. The loose end of the fluke chain is hauled inboard through a hawse hole in the forward bulwarks and made fast around the fluke bitt, at the bowsprit heel. Although under shortened sail, the ship retains enough headway to keep the whale close alongside, towing tail first. Cutting-in may now proceed, as the whale floats directly beneath the cutting stage.

Cutting off the head, the first operation, is exceedingly difficult and requires much skill. The whale is first turned on its side until the jaw faces the ship and is secured in that position. The officers then make an incision around the socket of the jaw by thrusting their cutting spades into the blubber, extending the cut around the eye in a semicircular curve to a point forward of the fin. The cutting tackle is lowered, one of the crew goes down on the whale and inserts the hook in the blanket piece, and the crew heave away on the windlass, the loosened blubber peeling off readily as the officers cut it clear at each side. As the blanket raises, the whale rolls slowly over until the jaw faces away from the ship, when the heaving is stopped.

The second cutting tackle is lowered and hooked into a chain strap slung over the jaw as the officers cut around the other socket and sever the throat, thrusting the spades down until they reach the backbone. The jaw, thus loosened, is then wrenched out and hoisted aboard as the blanket piece remains suspended by the other tackle.

The crew heave in more on the blanket piece until the whale is rolled right side up, when a chain strap is rove through the back part of the head, forming two loops. A fluke chain is passed through and drawn taut, while the other end is passed aboard through a hawse hole and made fast, thus securing the head when detached.

The whale is again rolled on its back and another strap rove through the front of the head. The tackle is hooked on and all hands heave on the windlass to facilitate separation from the skull bone. As the sperm whale has no real upper jaw, the skull bone takes its place. The whalemen on the stage now thrust their sharp spades along the edge of the skull as the enormous weight of the bulky mass hanging down opens the gash. The other tackle is slacked down, throwing the entire suspended weight upon the head, soon cleared from the bone by vigorous jabs of the cutting spades.

The incision around the throat is now deepened and the backbone unjointed, leaving the severed head attached to the ship by the chains previously rove through. This completes the most difficult part of the cutting-in process, and after securing the head farther aft removing the blubber proceeds.

The tackle hooked in the blanket piece, slacked away when cutting the head clear, is now hove up again and the huge blanket piece raised until the blocks meet at the lower masthead slings. The other tackle is lowered and hooked on at the gangway; the blanket piece is severed just above it, swung inboard and lowered into the blubber room down the hold.

The next blanket is stripped off, the heaving continues and the process repeated as the officers cut a spiral line around the whale as it rolls over and over. The blubber is thus removed until near the flukes, which are severed and allowed to slip through the fluke chain. The carcass, being of no value, is cast adrift to afford a feast for the ravenous sharks and sea birds that abound in the vicinity.

The head, the most valuable part of the whale, being almost a solid mass of blubber and spermaceti, is now brought opposite the gangway and subdivided, the entire mass being far too heavy to hoist in at one time. Even then its enormous weight taxes the strength of the tackle to its utmost and causes the ship to careen heavily.

Accordingly, the lower and heavier part, called the junk, is separated from the rest and taken in first, both tackles hooked on. It is then made fast by chains and ropes to prevent its becoming loose on deck by the rolling of the ship. The upper part, called the case, which contains the spermaceti, is either hoisted on board or level with the gangway, according to the size of the whale. Cutting-in now completed, the stage is hoisted in and the gangway section again placed in position.

Preparations are now made for trying out the blubber. Tryworks are cleared away and the fires started. The blubber, stowed below in the blubber room and piled on deck, is cut into strips called horse pieces and passed forward by the trypots where it is sliced or minced with mincing knives to be more easily tried out. The minced horse pieces are piled into the trypots, boiled out, and the scraps thrown into tubs to be used later as fuel.

Empty casks are hoisted on deck, coopered and lashed along the bulwarks. The oil is bailed into these after being cooled in the copper tank adjoining the tryworks. Meanwhile the "case" is slit open and the clear, snow-white spermaceti bailed or scooped out; the men plunging waist-deep in the pulpy, cellular ooze. When first removed it is quite fluid, but quickly congeals upon exposure to the air. After bailing out, it is thrown into the trypots and carefully heated to the proper temperature, when it is again cooled and drawn off into casks. The empty shell, a fibrous mass of muscles and tendons yielding no oil, is cast loose and allowed to slide overboard from the gangway at a favorable lurch of the ship. The "junk" is cut into horse pieces and tried out separately, the oil considered greatly superior to the rest; spermaceti, of course, being the most valuable.

Trying out proceeds without cessation day and night, half the crew working while the other watch is below. At night the ship presents a highly picturesque scene, the flames darting high above the tryworks, revealing spars and rigging in an uncanny glare. The crew, slipping and sliding about the deck, appear like demons capering about an incantation fire. However, with this picture the romance departs, for everything is drenched with oil that washes about, ankle deep, and the odor of burning scraps is beyond description. Smoke from the tryworks fires is choking in density, rigging and spars blackened, and reek with greasy soot from which there is no refuge.

It sometimes happens that more or less of the muscular, red whale meat adheres to the blubber when stripped off. This is called the "lean," and is carefully cut away and pitched into large open casks, where the sun and heat from the adjacent fires gradually drain out the oil. Being of inferior quality, this is tried out last, and the pieces unsuitable for the trypots sorted from the putrid mass and thrown overboard.

The Arctic bowhead whales were the most valuable, yielding whalebone of finest quality, the slabs in exceptional cases reaching a length of seventeen feet. These monster whales were thickly covered with blubber that yielded a large quantity of oil. Starbuck states that one has been known to produce 375 barrels of oil, 26 barrels being obtained from the tongue alone. The blubber on this whale was 2 feet in thickness, and the total weight of the 620 slabs of bone contained in the huge mouth was 3,000 pounds.

In cutting-in a bowhead or right whale, both species producing the whalebone of commerce, the process differs somewhat, although trying out is much the same. The upper part of the head containing the baleen or bone is hoisted in on deck and the slabs of bone, some four hundred or more according to size, are cut out with bone spades. These slabs form a sort of sieve or strainer hanging down on either side of the mouth, retaining the food from mouthfuls of water gathered by the whale as it swims along on the surface. The huge lower lips, practically solid fat, are severed and hoisted aboard separately, then cut up and boiled, as is the tongue. Afterward, stripping the carcass and trying out is similar to the procedure for sperm whales, although the oil is of much lower grade. Oil yielded by sperm whales was called sperm oil, but that from bowhead or right whales was termed "whale oil."

Trying out completed, the various implements are stowed away, the oil cooled and drawn off through canvas hose or pipes into casks below deck, and the ship cleared up ready for more whales, when the whole laborious process is repeated throughout the remainder of the voyage.

6. HOMEWARD BOUND
End of the Voyage

THERE were many abandoned whaling grounds in the different oceans, some from lack of whaling vessels to cruise there, and many because whales no longer haunted the spots that were once the favorite cruising grounds of the square rigger. The vast increase in number of steamships that ply the ocean over the very grounds where the whales sought their food, churning the waters and frightening the wary animals to other haunts less likely to become pathway for ocean greyhounds, was doubtless a vital factor.

Sometimes the voyage was made to the eastward to Tristan d'Acunha, past the Cape of Good Hope to the Crozets and north to Mozambique and Madagascar, and farther east to the shores of New Holland, as it was then known, now Australia. Thence around its southern shore to New Zealand and so into the west longitude in the Pacific and north to the Sandwich Islands, meeting the ships that had cruised around the Horn and burst stormingly into the great Southern Ocean. Northward in the Pacific, Mt. St. Elias in sight, then to the opposite coast of Kamchatka, through the fog and ice of Bering Strait or into the Okhotsk Sea. Point Barrow and farther east in the Arctic to Herschel Island, where they wintered amid the frozen, desolate waste of endless blizzards, ice and wintry desolation, suffering untold hardships.

It requires little imagination to realize the utter misery that must have been theirs. Not only did the whalemen have the dangerous ice floes to contend with, but frequently, when far away from fresh vegetables, the dread disease scurvy attacked a whole ship company. Taken altogether it was a cruel experience for hundreds of men who took the chance of making a few dollars. In one recorded instance fifteen men died of scurvy, just half the entire crew. During some winters men would wander away from the ships and were never heard from again.

Strange to say, these incidents were treated as merely commonplace and found slight mention in the ship log books, and the record of the most extraordinary achievements in discovery and adventure is likely to be a mere recounting of the wind, weather and sail carried, "and so ends" repeated to unending weariness and exasperation. The following entry, taken at random from the log of ship *Bengal,* is typical:

Monday March 14 1836 This 24 hours be gins with light brezes, from the East at 7 P.M. toock in saile for the night ships head two the S.S.E middle and later parts mutch the same as the first all saile out steering two the E.S.E Lat Obs 27° 0″ Long 33° 41″ East

Occasionally, however, the reader is rewarded and uncovers something of interest and sometimes importance. A reference to this effect is made by the *Morning Mercury,* of New Bedford, under date of March 4, 1938:

Old whaleship logs have taken on a new interest, since the United States Government has been conducting an intensive research into the history of some of the remote islands of the South Pacific Ocean, which have now come into new importance by reason of their potential value as air bases in the more extended air flight routes over the Pacific.

New Bedford whaleships cruising about the Pacific in search of whales stumbled upon some of these then uncharted islands, and for years the islands remained little known, except as they may have been visited by occasional ships. Masters of New Bedford whaleships were best acquainted with some of them, since they were a source of a supply of fresh water in an otherwise barren waste of salt water.

Howland Island, located in Latitude 0° 49' North, Longitude 176° 43' West, discovered in 1842 by Captain George E. Netcher, a New Bedford ship master, was named for George Howland, a New Bedford whaling merchant.

Captain Netcher's log book contains many interesting features, among which a number are worthy of note. On one occasion the captain was evidently considerably worried about the success of his voyage, for at the end of the record of the day's proceedings we find the following entry:

So Ends this 24 hours and we have seen two fin back whales and one schole of Black fish cins we have bin hear but i am in hopes two see some sperm whales and ketch them be fore long   George Netcher

Doubtless Captain Netcher's hopes were afterward realized, for a careful study of the log reveals that he made a tremendous voyage. However, it appears that trouble occasionally cropped up, and on Monday, December 14, 1835, he made the following entry:

This 24 hours be gins with hevey gailes from the West at 2 P.M toock in the foare and mizen topsail Ships head two the S.S.W middle parts more moderat at 9 A.M saw whales and goot redy two loare and all the peopel sed they would not gow in the boats be cus they was not yoused well for they did not have slush in the duff

Evidently the captain was something of a diplomat, for on the next day we find this entry:

This 24 hours be gins fresh brezes from the West at 2 P.M spock with the Ship Clay of Linn 9 whales at 3 P.M i maid out two let the crew two come on Deck by saying that they could have slush in the duff and small stores sutch as butter and chees and sow i didit rather than spoile

40

*mi voige middle and later parts fresh gailes from the N.W at 9 A.M
saw whales and loared waist boat struck and iron brock Lat 38" 25 South
Long 9" 40 East*

Unfortunately there were many occasions that arose requiring far more drastic treatment, for upon the high seas the master of a ship must also be master of his crew under any and all conditions, for the good of all concerned. The grim reality of what may have happened aboard the ship *Golconda* of Bristol, R.I., is indicated by Captain Netcher's log of the ship *Bengal,* under date of Thursday, March 31, 1836, as follows:

*This 24 hours be gins with light brezes from the West at 2 P.M spock
with the Ship Paladian and saw a Ship two the West stering East with
her colers set fore and aft and insen younion down 14 teen in mutnity
and Capten Chase put 4 of them in casks and 6 in irons and 4 he tied up
in the rigen Golconda—of Bristol R I at 6 A.M saw the land baring
East 30 miles later part calm Lat Obs 24" 10 S Long 42" 41 East*

The desperate situation that developed aboard the *Golconda* may readily be realized, for Captain Chase had been obliged to subdue fourteen men, practically half his crew, before he became master of the situation. There must have been a terrific struggle, and there seems little doubt that Captain Chase had an able crew of officers to support his authority.

After many tedious months that lengthened into years as a whaleship pursued her pathway at sea into the closing stages of a four-year voyage, the limited fare frequently becoming moldy and sodden with bilgewater and reeking with oil from the leaky casks, the hardy crew worn with endless toil under the broiling sun one season and half-frozen the next in icy latitudes, we may visualize the mental torment and misery that drove them to desperation.

There were other events at sea that cast their shadow over the ship, and in the log of bark *Dryade* of New Bedford, dated Saturday, September 15, 1832, we find the following:

This 24 hours begins with strong winds from the S.E. at P.M Doubble reefed the two topsailes at 4 P.M pumped Ship Forbes layes very low in dead J. Ball the same last part of this 24 hours come in with strong brezes from the S.E stering sharpe on the wind two the S.S.W at 4 A.M Marten Forbes died suposed two have bin poisoned at the cape Devirds at 8 A.M wore Ship two the N.E. by E bered the corpes Latitude 4.17 South Longitude by luner obs 22" 54" 45 West

So Ends

Under these and many other handicaps the business of the voyage proceeded: the leaky whaleships, strained and battered from the ceaseless battle against the elements, literally pumped their way around the world. Each whale taken brought them closer to the end of the voyage, and as the vision of a full ship with every cask stored below brought thoughts of home, the crews cheerfully shouldered the tasks before them.

Homeward bound! We can hardly realize what that meant to those rugged seamen, after suffering the hardships of their precarious calling through the many weary months that stretched into years since they cleared from port. Every morning at daylight, every day at noon and every evening, tacks, sheets, halyards, braces and bowlines are swayed home. After cruising about on the whaling grounds under shortened sail the bluff-bowed old ships took on a new lease of life as every stitch of canvas was spread to the breeze, for at last they were homeward bound, wallowing along through the rolling sea that never ceased to heave beneath their feet.

Making the landfall as they neared port, the green hills of Block Island brought tears of joy to their salt-burned eyes; and soon the friendly hail of the Cuttyhunk pilot greeted them, roaring across the wind "What ship is that?"

"The Ship *Bengal,* Netcher master, full to the hatches with sperm oil Come aboard!"

Every detail of the home port is eagerly absorbed as the ship creeps into the harbor, shortening sail for the last time as they swing into the wind and let go the anchor at quarantine. With flags fluttering from the mastheads, in a few more hours, formalities of inspection completed, a puffing tug eases the ship alongside the wharf, crowded with anxious friends, relatives and boarding-house runners. The scene is one of almost indescribable confusion; happy reunion for many, but despair and sorrow for those whose loved ones were buried at sea during the voyage.

Soon after arrival in port, cargo discharged and sail dried out, unbent and sent to the sail loft for repair and storage, the main and fore yards are cockbilled or swung to a forty-five degree angle and lashed. Topgallant and royal yards are sent down and topmasts housed, snugging the ship down for a rest in port before overhauling, to refit for sea and another voyage.

7. SETTLEMENT OF THE VOYAGE
The Profits of Whaling

THE customary method of settling whaling voyages was by a system of shares or "lays," as they were called, each officer and member of the crew being shipped to receive a stated proportion of the earnings as his share or payment, from which were deducted advances, various charges incurred before and during the voyage.

The fortunes of whaling were by no means always measured by the length of the voyage, as attested by that of the steam whaler *William Baylies* in 1905, when Captain H. H. Bodfish of Vineyard Haven brought his ship into port at San Francisco after an absence of but six months with a catch valued at $185,000. In November 1899, another steam whaler, the *Beluga,* after wintering north in the Arctic the previous season, arrived at San Francisco with the product of sixty-three whales taken in Mellville Bay. Although the price of whalebone had dropped at that time, the catch brought nearly $350,000.

Sperm whaling also proved highly profitable in those days. Captain Charles Grant of Nantucket, master of ship *Milton* of New Bedford on a voyage which terminated in 1869, forty-six months from port, brought a catch worth $250,000, the owners realizing a profit of more than $180,000.

The sperm whaling record made by the ship *Young Phoenix,* of New Bedford is notable. Covering the period between 1830 to 1878, the ship took 23,419 barrels of sperm oil, 9,488 barrels of whale oil, her combined cargoes bringing $1,096,000.

There are many instances on record of phenomenal catches by Yankee whalemen cruising in various parts of the world, from Nantucket, New London, Sag Harbor, Fairhaven, Bristol and other New England and north Atlantic ports.

Other whaling ventures were less fortunate, and many financial losses resulted from disaster and misfortune at sea. However, the average voyage was expected to yield a reasonable profit, and the following statement covering the settlement of a voyage of whaleship *Milton* of New Bedford will prove of interest, as it gives the lay of every member of the crew and the amount credited to them from proceeds of the voyage.

SETTLEMENT OF VOYAGE, SHIP MILTON, 1836.

LIST OF SHIP MILTON CREW AND THEIR SHARES.

Name	Rating	Lay	Share
Robert Tuckerman	Master	1/17	$5,882
Ezra T. Howland	Mate	1/22	4,545
Charles T. Terry	2nd mate	1/50	2,000
Antone Mays	3d mate	1/65	1,538
Archilaus Baker 3d	Boatsteerer	1/75	1,333
Samuel N. Brush	ditto	1/90	1,111
Charles D. Dyke	ditto	1/85	1,176
Benjamin F. Hatch	Cooper	1/50	2,000
Clark Morse	2nd ditto	1/150	666
William Sholes	Carpenter	1/110	909
Adam Mackie	Steward	1/175	591
Robert Elliot	Cook	1/115	869
Jesse Munson	Seaman	1/125	800

William Thompson	Seaman	1/130	$769
John Blooming	ditto	1/120	833
George Williams	ditto	1/125	800
John Corey	ditto	1/125	800
William H. Marsh	Ord. Seaman	1/175	571
James McCully	Blacksmith	1/140	714
Albert N. Buttz	Landsman	1/190	526
John C. Morse	ditto	1/180	555
William Graves	ditto	1/175	571
Edward Griffin	ditto	1/175	571
John Alexander	ditto	1/175	571
William P. Hatch	ditto	1/220	454
Henry Jackson	ditto	1/175	571
John Scott	ditto	1/175	571

There were many occasions when profits to the crew proved deeply disappointing, sometimes partly due to misfortunes of the voyage and perhaps too-liberal purchases of clothing and supplies from the slop chest, or cash advances previous to departure. The low watermark of all time seems to belong to one John Murray, ordinary seaman, ship *Milton,* 1844. The following is taken from the book containing the settlements of this ship's voyages over a period of years, and is an exact copy of the receipt acknowledged by Mr. Murray.

New Bedford 5 m 25, 1844   Received of Henry Taber & Co. ten cents balance due me for my late voyage in Ship Milton and also Ten dollars in cash and for which I release said Ship Capt Lewis and officers from all claims & demands.   his
                              John ✕ Murray
                              mark

The details of the account against Mr. Murray are:—"To amount ship's bill, $25.05; share of medicine chest, .42; discharging ship 1.50; Cook & Snow bill, 32.73. The balance of ten cents made his share $59.80, being his lay of 1/160 on an amount stated $9,568."

Yet the Yankee whalemen were a thrifty people and made splendid citizens, saving their earnings and building comfortable homes wherein to reside during the remainder of their days after retirement from the sea. The palatial residences at Nantucket, New Bedford and other whaling ports were a tribute to the more successful whaling masters and merchants who built mansions of credit and example to their home community.

Whaling still went on for years. Strange as it seems, during the closing days of the whale fishery methods of conducting the industry differed little from those in practice a century before, and although bomb lances, darting and shoulder guns for killing whales were introduced, they never displaced the hand lances and harpoons.

Although the bowhead, right and sperm whale fisheries have been abandoned by American ships, Norwegian steamers equipped as floating rendering-plants cruise the southern seas and produce large quantities of low-grade oil and fertilizer products from finback, humpback and sulphur bottom whales that still abound in the Antarctic.

The quaint, bluff-bowed old craft from New Bedford, with their curious carved eagles and figureheads, after plowing the seas a half-century or more have given up the chase, and left the sperm whale still monarch of the deep.

Part Two

ILLUSTRATIONS

*1. The New Bedford waterfront as it appeared in 1878, when arrival
and departure of whaleships from all parts of the world were almost
a daily occurrence. On the docks in the foreground are hundreds of
casks filled with sperm and whale oil, covered with seaweed to prevent
exposure to the sun and consequent loss from leakage.*

2. *Whaling brig* VIOLA *building at Essex, Mass., in 1910, showing rugged construction of frames, keelson and ceiling.*

3. Building VIOLA, *view on deck looking aft, showing angle irons for tryworks and planking for the goose pen before brickwork is begun.*

4. *Looking forward, showing windlass in position.*

5. *Port quarter view, hull completed.*

6. *Bow view of* VIOLA, *ready to launch.*

7. *Windlass barrel, being turned on hand lathe.*

8. *The old spar shop, showing spar roughed out ready for rounding.*

9. *Heaving down a whaleship, showing the windlass and arrangement of blocks attached to the heaving post.*

10. *An old heaving down post.*

11. *Ship* JAMES ARNOLD *hove down for repairs.*

12. Bow view of bark JOSEPHINE *hove down, keel out.*

13. Resheathing the garboard. bark MORNING STAR.

14. *Coating the bottom with hot pitch before laying felt base, sheathing and copper.*

15. *Hull partially sheathed, lower strakes completed.*

16. *Caulking the seams.*

17. *Ship carpenters fitting the pine sheathing.*

18. Repairing the quarter timbers, bark SUNBEAM.

19. *Bark* WANDERER, *hauled out on the railway.*

19. *Bark* WANDERER, *hauled out on the railway.*

20. *Starboard bow view, bark* CHARLES W. MORGAN *on the ways.*

21. Bark ANDREW HICKS *undergoing repairs, showing the unusual carved sternboard decoration.*

22. *Bow view of bark* WANDERER *on the ways, showing carved eagle figurehead.*

23. *Bark* ANDREW HICKS, *recoppered, ready to launch.*

24. *Paying the seams after caulking, bark* GREYHOUND.

25. *Rigging the jibboom,*
CHARLES W. MORGAN.

26. *The boss rigger, at the right, overseeing his men as they prepare to run out the jibboom and set up the head rigging.*

27. Painting the billet, bark BERTHA.

28. Figurehead, bark ALICE KNOWLES, *built in Weymouth, 1879.*

29. Detail of carved billet, bark PLATINA.

30. Sternboard from brig EUNICE H. ADAMS, *last whaler from Edgartown.*

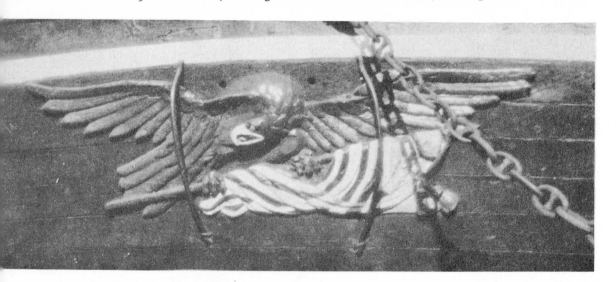

31. Carved eagle sternboard, bark MORNING STAR.

32. Pilaster capital for whaleship's cabin, carved by Henry Purrington of Mattapoisett, Mass. Mr. Purrington carved the billets, fiddleheads, figureheads, trail boards and sternboards of many whaleships, including the eagle stempiece and cabin decoration of bark WANDERER.

33. *Building a whaleboat. Planked up.*

34. *Boat nearly completed, showing ceiling and centerboard trunk.*

35. *New whaleboats for shipment to whalers at the Azores.*

36. *Hooping knockdown oil casks, called "shooks," a method employed to economize stowage aboard ship.*

37. *Repairing oil casks and hoops when fitting out.*

38. *Demolishing tryworks before rebuilding.*

39. *Laying the ground tier of brickwork inside the goose pen.*

40. *250 gallon trypot, before resetting.*

41. *Tryworks well under way; setting the trypots.*

42. *Iron grate bars in position under the trypots.*

43. *Bricking in the trypots.*

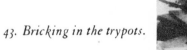

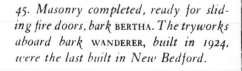

44. *Nearly bricked in, showing the iron sheathing outside.*

45. *Masonry completed, ready for sliding fire doors, bark* BERTHA. *The tryworks aboard bark* WANDERER, *built in 1924, were the last built in New Bedford.*

46. *Whalecraft and gear as brought from warehouse. Harpoons, lances, cutting blocks, etc., ready to go aboard.*

47. *Cord wood, cutting stage, cooper's bench, fluke chains, blubber hook and oil casks, ready to go aboard the bark* ALICE KNOWLES, *refitting.*

48. *Bringing sails from sail loft, cutting blocks in foreground. Note strength of the heavy tackle.*

49. *Sails aboard brig* DAISY, *ready to bend.*

50. *Overhauling fluke chains and ground tackle.*

51. *Cutting blocks aloft, bark*
WANDERER.

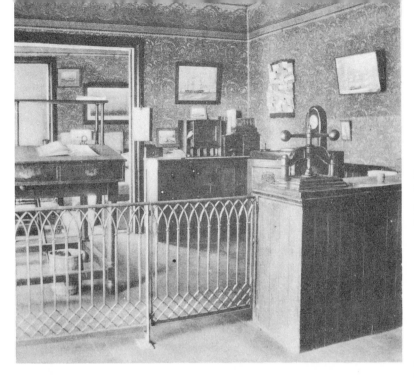

52. *The old shipping office or counting house of Swift & Allen, whaling merchants, New Bedford.*

53. *Master rigger Peter Black, last of the old time riggers.*

54. *Last of the shipsmiths, maker of whalecraft, Edward R. Cole at the old forge in Fairhaven, Mass.*

The original metal pattern used by Mr. Cole for many years from which harpoon heads, such as those to the right, were cast of malleable iron. Formerly harpoons were forged entirely by hand; the harpoons, lances and spades being referred to as whalecraft. When malleable cast heads were introduced the shipsmith was only required to forge the iron shaft and socket for the handle or pole, which was usually made of hickory.

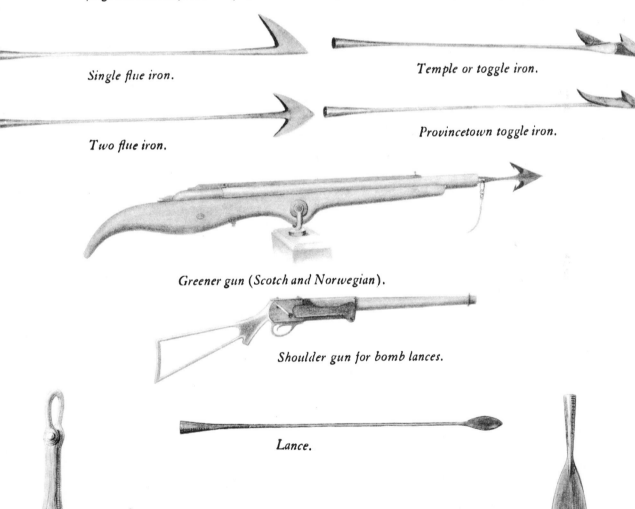

Single flue iron.

Temple or toggle iron.

Two flue iron.

Provincetown toggle iron.

Greener gun (Scotch and Norwegian).

Shoulder gun for bomb lances.

Lance.

Blubber hook.

Cutting spade.

55. WHALECRAFT.

56. *View on deck, ship ready for sea, crowded with visitors and friends of the crew.*

57. *Old-fashioned whaleship's dry compass, made by C. R. Sherman, of New Bedford.*

58. *Whaling bark* BERTHA, *ready for sea.*

59. *The full-rigged whaleship* HORATIO, *of New Bedford, ready for sea. The* HORATIO, *built by James M. Bayles & Son at Port Jefferson, L.I. in 1877, was considered one of the finest ships in the fleet.*

In the foreground may be seen the heaving post to which the huge blocks and tackle were attached when heaving down a whaleship for recoppering and repairs.

60. *The captain inspects the ship,* schooner JOHN R. MANTA.

61. *Belated members of the crew are rounded up.*

62. *Friends taking leave of crew as ship lies in the stream.*

63. *Colors flying, last Sunday in port.*

64. *Ship towing into the stream to await arrival of crew before departure.*

65. Clear of the docks, the whaleboats are hoisted on the davits and made ready for sea.

66. *The crew all aboard, the anchor is broken out and the ship leaves the harbor in tow.*

67. *As the ship clears the headlands, sails are loosened to the breeze.*

68. *Topsails and topgallant sails sheeted home.*

69. Leaving New Bedford astern, bark WANDERER.

70. *Plunging into a head sea, bark* MORNING STAR.

71. *The* MORGAN *casts off the hawser.*

72. Owners and guests leave the ship.

73. Whaleboat returning guests to tug.

74. After ferrying guests to the tug, the whaleboat returns—is hoisted on the davits, and the ship is off on her voyage.

75. *Bark* CHARLES W. MORGAN *awaits a breeze.*

76. *Yards aback, braced around, bark* CANTON *proceeds to sea.*

77. *The* MORGAN *picks up the breeze.*

78. The MORGAN *under full sail, showing three whaleboats on the port side.*

79. *The* CHARLES W. MORGAN, *from off the starboard quarter, showing the cutting stage rigged opposite the gangway. It is from this stage, when lowered down parallel with the sea level, that whales are cut in alongside the ship, always on the starboard side.*

80. *Starboard side of the* MORGAN.

81. *From off the port bow.*

82. *Brig* VIOLA *bound to sea on her first voyage.*

83. *Three-masted schooner whaler,* MYSTIC.

84. *The* MORGAN *aback*.

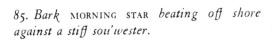

85. *Bark* MORNING STAR *beating off shore against a stiff sou'wester.*

86. WANDERER *before the wind.*

87. *Off on the voyage.*

88. *Reflections on the sea.*

89. The captain watches the fading shore as the JOSEPHINE *proceeds to sea.*

90. Bark CHARLES W. MORGAN *sails on her last voyage.*

91. WANDERER, *a bone in her teeth.*

92. *The full-rigged whaleship* JAMES ARNOLD, *built at New Bedford in 1852, leaving port in 1894. The frequent reference to the* JAMES ARNOLD *in the specifications for construction of the ship* HORATIO *indicates she was considered a splendid example of her type, both in model and construction. This beautiful photograph was taken by Mr. J. Arnold Wright of New Bedford.*

The JAMES ARNOLD, *Captain Sullivan, when whaling off New Zealand, took in one voyage eight whales that made more than 100 barrels each, the largest yielding 137 barrels. The head made 52 barrels and the case bailed 27 barrels. The flukes were 18 feet across, jaw 18 feet long, case 22 feet, and the forehead 12½ feet high. The total length of the big sperm was 90 feet.*

93. Schooner WILLIAM A. GROZIER *cruising on the Hatteras grounds, lookout aloft watching for whales.*

94. *Whaleboat and gear complete, line tubs in foreground.*

95. *Drilling greenhand boat's crew during calm weather.*

96. Lowered for whales, setting sail in the boat.

97. Going on the whale, ready to give him the iron. From a painting by Raleigh.

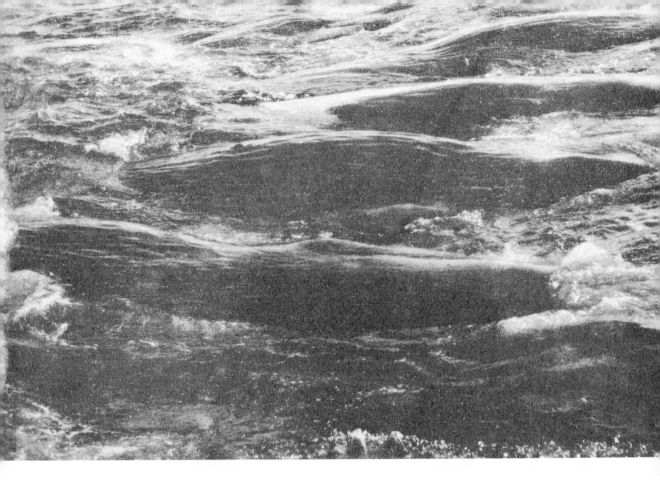

98. *Five whales alongside, ready to cut in.*

99. *Bark* CATALPA, *cutting-in a large sperm whale alongside, showing the arrangement of cutting blocks and falls. From a painting made by Raleigh many years ago. The crew may be seen forward heaving on the windlass, and it will be noted the old-fashioned double cutting stage was in use at that period. The longer single stage afterward used was a great improvement, as several men could work on a large whale at the same time.*

100. *Cutting-in a sperm whale. The whale is rolled on its back as the jaw is cut away and wrenched out.*

101. Taking in the 25-foot jaw of a huge sperm whale, bark CHARLES W. MORGAN.

102. The "overboard man," preparing to reeve the head chain through before severing the head. An especially dangerous task in heavy weather.

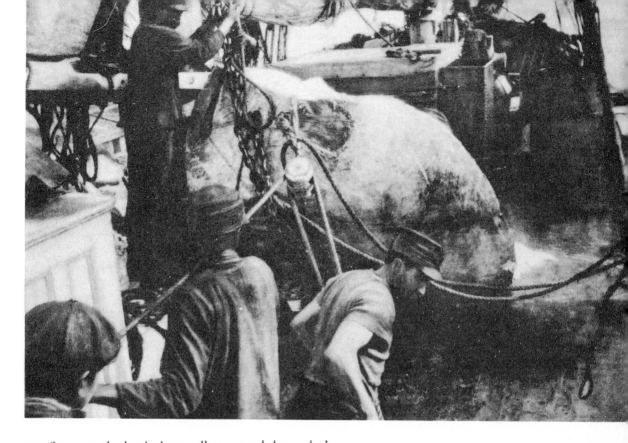

103. *Securing the head of a small sperm whale on deck.*

104. *The junk of a large sperm whale aboard, at left, the case hoisted up level with planksheer ready for bailing.*

105. *Bailing the case. The case is slit open and the valuable spermaceti bailed or scooped out into large tubs.*

106. *Heads of two right whales, a cow and calf, taken by the* CHARLES W. MORGAN *in the Indian Ocean.*

The slabs of bone that separate the small brit and shrimp upon which the whale feeds when swimming along on the surface, may be clearly seen. The huge lower lips swing outward as the whale swims along, closing snugly against the slabs of bone within the mouth when sufficient water containing the tiny morsels of food has been taken in. Raising the enormous tongue, the whale forces the water outward through the natural sieve or strainer of whale-bone, the brit and shrimp becoming enmeshed by the slabs of bone and the thick, wiry hair at the lower extremity. The food remaining after expelling the water is then swallowed.

107. *Whale cut in, ready for slicing the blubber, schooner* JOHN R. MANTA.

108. *Blankets of blubber being cut into horse pieces, cooper's bench and tryworks in background.*

109. *Sliced blubber on deck, three-masted whaling schooner* ARTHUR V. S. WOODRUFF.

110. Mincing the horsepieces.

111. Tryworks in operation, ARTHUR V. S. WOODRUFF.

112. Skimming the scraps, which are fed to the fires as fuel.

113. Ship NIGER *of New Bedford, built at Mattapoisett in 1844. From a negative made by William Bradford, about 1880.*

114. *Cutting spades all sharpened, the cooper takes time out.*

115. *"Come an' get it," a welcome sound aboard ship.*

116. *Captain Henry Mandley of the* MANTA *ready to shoot the sun.*

117. *Quarter-deck of the* MANTA, *riding out a gale on the Hatteras grounds.*

118. *Blackfish brought to port for trying out.*

119. *The head of a three-ton blackfish, showing the upper portion of the head, called the melon.*

120. *Group of blackfish heads from which the melon has been removed.*

121. *Strips of blackfish blubber ready for slicing or mincing.*

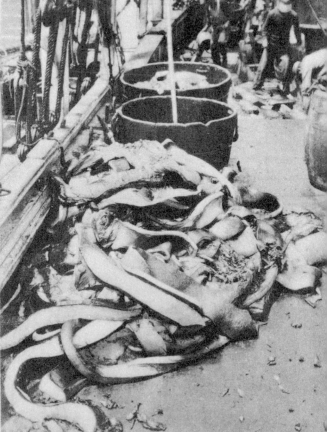

122. Slicing the blackfish blubber.

123. Trying out blackfish aboard the schooner ELLEN A. SWIFT.

124. Bark MORNING STAR *returning from a voyage. From a negative by Mr. W. W. Hill.*

125. Ship JAMES ARNOLD, *arriving in port, about 1885.*

126. Arrival of bark STAFFORD.

127. *Whaling schooner* CLAUDIA, *in from a voyage.*

128. *Schooner* MARGARETT, *lying at quarantine with a full cargo.*

129. *Bark* CHARLES W. MORGAN, *just arrived, her whaleboats alongside. Whalers at the right are brig* DAISY *and bark* ALICE KNOWLES.

130. *Bark* A. R. TUCKER, *built at Dartmouth in 1851, 138 tons register, was one of the smallest whalers in the fleet.*

131. WANDERER *discharging her cargo.*

132. *The* WANDERER, *a study in sunlight and shadow.*

133. *Bark* GREYHOUND, *built at New Bedford in 1851, completes her final whaling voyage, forced by a serious leak to leave the grounds. While trying to cut in a whale during heavy weather, the strain opened the seams under the port main chain plates and the crew were obliged to pump night and day to save the ship. Oil casks and heavy chain were moved as far forward as possible to raise the leak for the temporary canvas patch, which can be seen at the waterline. The vessel at the right is the schooner* JOHN R. MANTA.

134. WANDERER, *just arrived, drying sail.*

135. The MORGAN *returns from her final voyage, May, 1921.*

136. *Bark* ALICE KNOWLES *returns to New Bedford after 20 years' whaling in the Pacific and Arctic oceans. During this period she refitted at San Francisco.*

137. *A once familiar sight from New Bedford harbor.*

138. Bark CHARLES W. MORGAN *carried a main royal in 1908.*

139. Riggers aloft.   *140. Unbending canvas.*

141. Whaleboats.

142. *Hoisting out the oil casks.*

143. *Bark* KATHLEEN, *of New Bedford, was sunk by a whale a thousand miles off the coast of Brazil in March, 1902. Two other instances of this kind are on record. Whaleship* ESSEX *was sunk by a sperm whale in 1819, and the ship* ANN ALEXANDER *was sunk in the Pacific on August 20, 1851, latitude 5°50′ S, longitude 102°00′ W.*

144. *The* WANDERER *drying out her canvas.*

145. *Pumping out casks and gauging the oil.*

146. *Ship* MILTON, *of New Bedford, showing stevedore Frank Lewis, an experienced whaleman, and longshoremen storing casks of oil awaiting favorable market.*

147. Four whalers in port. Left to right, three-masted schooner MYSTIC, *bark* GREY-HOUND *and schooners* WILLIAM A. GROZIER *and* JOHN R. MANTA.

148. Three square-rigged whalers laid up in port. Barks A. R. TUCKER *and* SUNBEAM; *brig* DAISY, *sea elephant hunter, at the right.*

149. *Ship* ELIZA ADAMS *and bark* STAFFORD, *about 1885.*

150. CHARLES W. MORGAN, *dismantled, at Fairhaven.*

151. Bark JANET, about 1875, showing the finely carved sternboard.

152. Whaleboat, stove by flukes of a whale, too badly damaged for repair on shipboard.

153. Bark DESDEMONA *dismantled, before refitting. She was afterward lost at sea.*

154. Bow of the COMMODORE MORRIS, *one of the most famous old type whalers, showing her figurehead, one of the finest examples of its kind.*

155. Famous old whaleships ROUSSEAU *and* DESDEMONA. *Bark* ROUSSEAU *(left), was built in 1801 at Philadelphia for Stephen Girard, and was broken up at New Bedford in 1893 after many years service as a whaleship. Under ship rig originally, she appears as a whaler in the North Pacific fishery in the records of 1834. The* DESDEMONA, *built at Middletown in 1823, was also ship-rigged when built.* ROUSSEAU, *with the graceful curved head timbers and carved billet, and* DESDEMONA *with the splendid figurehead, were two of the most beautiful ships sailing from New Bedford.*

156. Type of whaleships built 50 years later, WANDERER *and* ANDREW HICKS.

157. *Old Provincetown whaler* ANTARCTIC, *ready to be broken up at New Bedford.*

158. *Between decks, bark* COMMODORE MORRIS, *showing the wooden cooling tank.*

159. Breaking up the old bark COMMODORE MORRIS.

160. Ship carpenters preparing to reship rudder.

161. Bark CHARLES W. MORGAN *at sea homeward bound, July 4th, 1908, from a photograph by Wm. H. Briggs.*

162. Bark PLATINA *at Merrills' Wharf, 1912.*

163. Sails brailed up ready to unbend.

164. Sails hang limp in the idle breeze.

165. *Reviving an old custom, Chaplain Thurber of the Seaman's Bethel gives the benediction aboard the* WANDERER *on the Sunday before she sails on her last voyage.*

166. *Visitors aboard the bark, last Sunday in port.*

167. *The* WANDERER *is towed out into the stream. Captain Edwards and mate are in the foreground.*

168. Bark WANDERER, *built at Mattapoisett, Mass., in 1878, was the last square-rigged whaleship to sail from New Bedford. She sailed on August 25, 1924, and was wrecked the following day on Cuttyhunk Island during a severe northeasterly gale that swept the Atlantic coast.*

169. The seas batter the hull of the WANDERER *on the rocks at Cuttyhunk.*

170. The end of a famous whaleship.

171. WANDERER'S *rudder found a quarter of a mile down the beach.*

172. Bark CHARLES W. MORGAN, *starboard broadside showing detail of rigging.*

173. CHARLES W. MORGAN *at the time of her dedication at Round Hills, Mass., flying the house flags of former New Bedford whaling merchants.*

174. *Bow as seen from aloft showing windlass.*

175. *One of the* MORGAN'S *old anchors. showing cathead.*

176. *The* MORGAN'S *windlass.*

177. *Mizzen mast, bark rig, forward side.*   178. *Mizzen mast, bark rig, starboard side.*

179. *Mizzen mast, ship rig.*   180. *Mizzen channels, bark rig.*

181. *After side of main mast.*

182. *After side of main mast, showing details of topgallant mast.*

183. *Starboard side of main mast.*

184. *Forward side of main mast, ready for sea, showing masthead loops for lookouts in position above main topgallant truck.*

185. *After side of main mast from port side, showing close up detail of main truck and shrouds.*

186. *Starboard side of main mast and main topmast.*

187. *Main channels and chain plates. Cooper's anvil and scrap tubs in foreground.*

188. *Starboard side of foremast and foretop mast.*

189. *After side of foremast, showing foretop-mast and foretopgallant mast ready for sea.*

190. *Forward side of foremast, showing close-up detail of truck.*

191. Fore channels and chain plates.

192. Removable gangway, starboard side, looking aft.

193. Cabin skylight.

194. The dining table, main cabin.

195. The MORGAN's *wheel, front elevation.*

196. The MORGAN's *wheel, side view, showing arrangement of traveling tiller and wheel ropes.*

197. The MORGAN *hauled out on the railways for repair.*

198. *Bow section view*, CHARLES W. MORGAN.

199. *Starboard bow.*

200. *Stern of the* MORGAN.

201. *The* MORGAN's *fiddlehead or billet.*

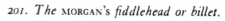

202. *The* MORGAN *as she appeared at Round Hills, Mass., after her single topsail ship rig was restored (1925).*

203. *The* MORGAN'S *original sternboard, afterwards lost at sea off the coast of Africa.*

204. The MORGAN at Round Hills, Mass., after weathering the hurricane of September 21st, 1938. Although the terrific seas crashed over the ship for hours and raised her six feet or more from her bed of sand, the only damage sustained was the loss of the eagle sternboard, a narrow strip of planking from the port quarter, and most of the copper sheathing, washed away by the continuous pounding of the seas. Nothing was carried away aloft.

205. The MORGAN's port quarter after the hurricane, showing the narrow strip of planking carried away, at the right just below the painted port. This was the only structural damage to the 97-year-old hull.

206. The MORGAN's eagle sternboard, placed in position in 1925, was swept away by the hurricane. Her original eagle was lost during a hurricane off the coast of Africa about 1910, when the three boats on the port davits were also carried away.

Part Three

WHALESHIP PLANS AND SPECIFICATIONS

Data on the Vessels Illustrated

Name	rig	tons	length	beam	depth	when built	
ALICE							
KNOWLES	bark	302.78	115.0	28.0	16.7	1879	Weymouth
ANDREW HICKS	bark	303.12	111.3	27.1	15.7	1867	Westport
ARTHUR V. S.							
WOODRUFF	sch (3m)	193.	105.6	27.1	10.3	1888	Essex
A. R. TUCKER	bark	138.09	92.4	23.2	11.0	1851	Dartmouth
BERTHA	bark	177.37	99.6	25.7	11.5	1878	New Bedford
CANTON	bark	238.82	103.1	24.8	15.4	1835	Baltimore
CAPE HORN							
PIGEON	bark	212.02	100.0	24.9	14.4	1854	Dartmouth
CHARLES W.							
MORGAN	bark	314.	105.6	27.7	17.6	1841	New Bedford
COMMODORE							
MORRIS	bark	338.21	107.	27.7	17.9	1841	Falmouth
CONTEST	ship	341.	118.	28.	14.	1856	Mattapoisett
DESDEMONA	bark	287.89	98.6	26.6	14.7	1823	Middletown
ELIZA ADAMS	ship	408.34	111.8	28.5	19.5	1835	Fairhaven
GREYHOUND	bark	177.89	95.0	24.4	12.2	1851	New Bedford
HORATIO	ship	349.03	115.7	28.6	17.5	1877	Port Jefferson
JAMES ARNOLD	ship	345.84	115.2	27.6	17.6	1852	New Bedford
JANET	bark	154.				1845	Portland
JOHN R.							
MANTA	sch	149.0	101.8	24.9	10.2	1904	Essex
JOSEPHINE	bark	384.54	129.7	29.0	17.2	1877	Bath
KATHLEEN	bark	205.51	104.	25.2	12.5	1844	Philadelphia
MARGARETT	sch	138.0	92.2	22.7	8.8	1889	Essex
MORNING STAR	bark	238.09	104.6	25.6	15.1	1853	Dartmouth

Name	rig	tons	length	beam	depth	when built	
MYSTIC	sch (3m)	259.0	123.0	30.1	10.7	1908	Mystic
NIGER	ship	411.69	116.6	29.2	19.2	1844	Mattapoisett
PLATINA	bark	214.27	94.0	25.3	15.2	1847	Mattapoisett
ROUSSEAU	bark	305.46	92.9	28.3	18.3	1801	Philadelphia
STAFFORD	bark	156.0	93.3	23.6	10.5	1848	Kingston
SUNBEAM	bark	255.31	106.4	27.3	15.2	1856	Mattapoisett
VIOLA	brig	190.0	125.0	26.1	12.5	1910	Essex
WANDERER	bark	303.28	116.0	27.0	15.0	1878	Mattapoisett
WILLIAM A. GROZIER	sch	117.0	91.0	22.0	8.0	1873	Kennebunk-port

206. RIGHT.

A Greenland right whale was taken in 1813 measuring 67 feet in length and 40 feet in circumference. In 1861 the GENERAL PIKE, *of New Bedford, took a whale on the Kodiah grounds that stowed down 274 barrels of oil.*

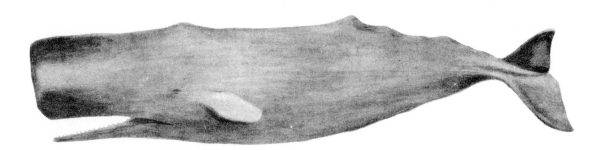

207. SPERM.

In 1876 bark WAVE *of New Bedford reported to have taken a sperm whale that made 162 barrels and 5 gallons of oil.*

The OCMULGEE *of Edgartown took a sperm whale in 1862 that stowed down 130 barrels whose jaw measured 28 feet in length.*

Sperm whales that yield 100 barrels are considered very large, but this yield was often exceeded.

208. SULPHUR BOTTOM.

The sulphur bottom whale is of the finback species, often reaching large size, some having been known to yield from 130 to 160 barrels of oil. They usually run when struck, as does the regular finback, and frequently sink after finning out dead. Their spout resembles a sperm whale's, but they differ in shape, having no hump, and are much longer.

Beale gives actual measurement of 84 feet, others taken have reached 95 feet in length and 39 feet girth.

#11

#12

Scale ½ in to 1 foot.

209. Sailmaker's Plan for Whaling Bark SUNBEAM, 1856.

Main Spencer Gaff, 15 feet whole length, one foot ends. Spritsail yard,
  17½ feet

Foremast, 57¼ feet long, 20″ at partners, head 10′
Foretopmast, 36 feet long, 12½″ at cap
Foretopgallantmast, 37 feet long, 8″ at cap
Mainmast, 59 feet 10 inches long, 22″ at partners, head 10 ft.
Maintopmast, 36 feet, 12½″ at cap
Maintopgallantmast, 37 feet long, 8″ at cap
Mizzenmast, 60 feet long, 16″ at partners

Mizzen topmast, 53 feet, 9¼ at cap
Fore and Main Yards, 54 feet, 3 foot ends, 13½ diameter
Fore and Maintopsail yards, 44 feet long, 3½ foot ends, 11″ d.
Foretopgallant and maintopgallant yards, 32 feet, 2½ ends, 7½″ diameter
Fore and main royal yards, 23 feet, 1½ ends, 5 inches diameter
Spanker Boom, 31 feet whole length, 18 inch ends
Spanker Gaff, 28 feet overall, 6 foot ends
Jib Boom, 17 feet inboard, 16 feet, 11 feet, 3 feet outboard

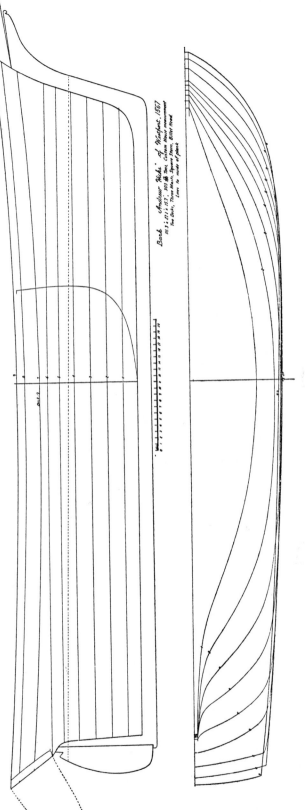

Bark Andrew Hicks of Westport. 1867
111.3 : 27.1 : 15.7 . 303 13/100 Tons. Custom House measurement
Two Decks, Three Masts, Square Stern, Billet Head.
Lines to inside of plank

210. Lines of Bark ANDREW HICKS of Westport, 1867.

111′ 3″ x 27′ 1″ x 15′ 7″, 303 13/100 tons, Custom House measurement. Two decks, three masts, square stern, Billet head. Lines to inside of plank.

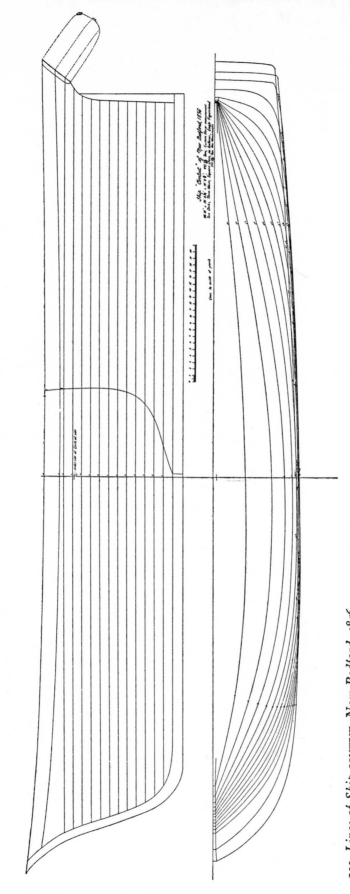

211. *Lines of Ship* CONTEST, *New Bedford, 1856.*

118′ 10″ x 28′ 8¾″ x 14′ 4¹¹/₁₂″, 441²²/₉₅ tons, Custom House measurement. Two decks, three masts, square stern, no galleries, Eagle figurehead, 341⁶⁴/₁₀₀ tons new measurement. Lines to inside of plank.

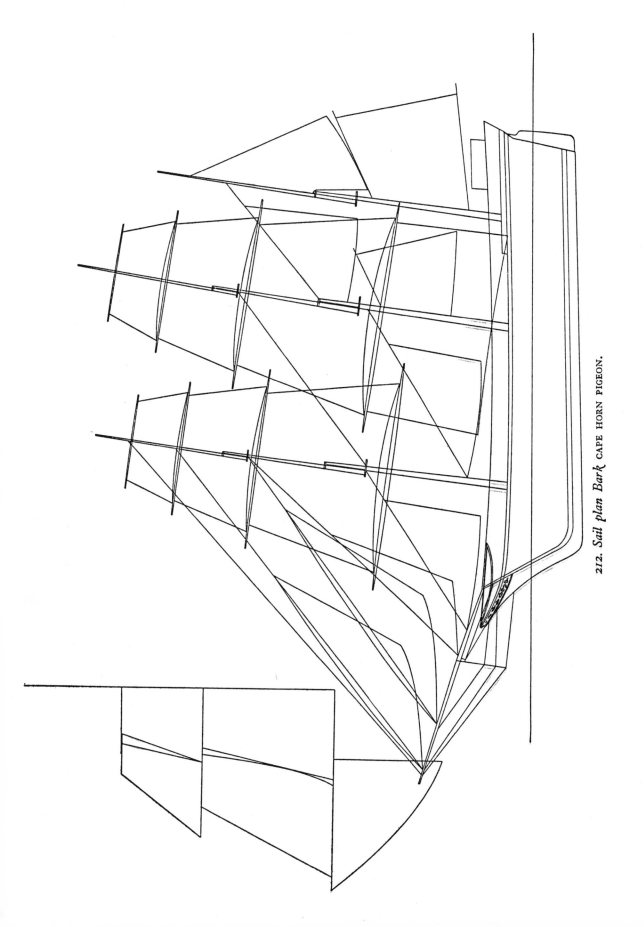

212. Sail plan Bark CAPE HORN PIGEON.

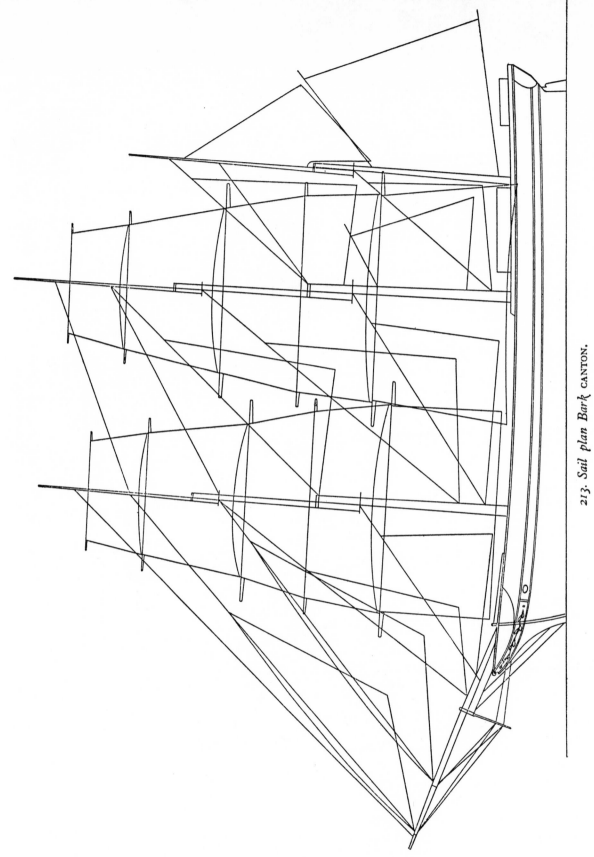

213. *Sail plan Bark* CANTON.

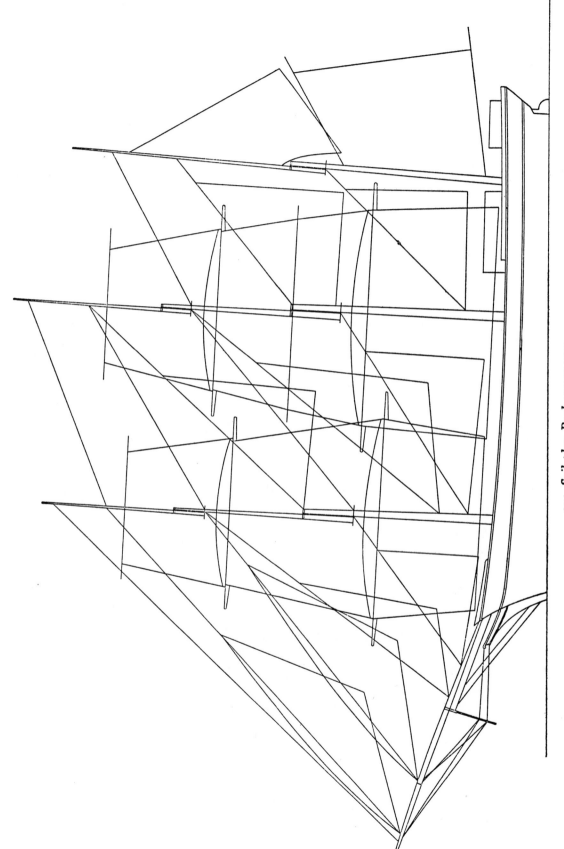

214. *Sail plan Bark* DESDEMONA.

SPECIFICATIONS FOR WHALESHIP *HORATIO*

AND CONTRACT

BETWEEN

JAMES M. BAYLES & SON BUILDERS

AND

TABER, GORDON & CO. OWNERS

DECEMBER 18,

1876

THIS agreement made and entered into the 18th day of December 1876 by and between James M. Bayles & Son of Port Jefferson, Suffolk County State of New York, party of the first part, and Taber Gordon & Co. of New Bedford, State of Massachusetts, party of the second part. Witnesseth.

That the said party of the first part agrees for themselves, their heirs or assigns together with the said party of the second part, their heirs or assigns, to build and construct rightly and properly for the said party of the second part, a ship for the Whaling service of the Dimensions Materials and Finish as here after described.

DIMENSIONS. To be 103 feet Keel from half of scarf of stem to after side of Stern Post. To be 27⁹⁄12 feet wide moulded, in the widest place, and to be 17 feet deep, measuring from top of ceiling to under side of upper deck in the main hatch.

KEEL. To be of White Oak 12½ by 18 inches with a false keel 6 by 12½ inches.

STEM. To be White Oak sided 12 inches.

STERN POST. To be White Oak to side 10 inches at bottom and 14 inches at transom.

APRON. To be Live Oak and side 18 inches.

TRANSOM. To be Live Oak and side 12 to 14 inches.

KNIGHT HEADS. And side counter timbers to be Live Oak of suitable sizes.

FRAMES. To be White Oak, Locust, Yellow Pine and Hackmatack, to mould 12 inches at keel and 5½ inches at upper decks.

KEELSONS. To be Yellow Pine. Main Keelson 14 by 14 inches and rider 12 by 12 inches.

CEILING. To be 3 inches thick on floor of Yellow Pine.

174

BILGE STREAKS. To have 5 Streaks in bilge 4 or 4½ inches thick of Yellow Pine.
CLAMPS. To have two streaks of Clamps under deck frame of Yellow Pine 4 or 5 inches thick. Between Clamps and bilge streaks to be 3 inches thick of Yellow Pine. To have an air streak 3½ inches wide below Clamps.
LOWER DECK FRAME. Beams to side 12 inches and mould 12 inches in center and 9 inches at the ends. Carlins to be 6 by 8 inches with fore and
AFT. aft pieces 10 by 7 inches, all to be Yellow Pine.
PARTNERS. To be 10 (8) inches thick as wide as necessary of Yellow Pine save those in Main Deck and Lower Deck which are to be of Oak.
LOWER DECK PLANK. To be of Yellow Pine, 3 by 8, 9, or 10 inches.
KNEES. To be Hackmatack 7 inches thick to be double Kneed at each end of the beams.
WATERWAYS. To be one streak 5 inches thick on beam ends.
CEILING BETWEEN DECKS. Streak above that 4 inches thick from thence to upper Clamps to be ceiled with 3 inches, all of Yellow Pine.
UPPER CLAMPS. To have two streaks 4 inches thick with an air streak 3 inches wide under Clamps, all to be of Yellow Pine.
UPPER DECK BEAMS. To side 12 inches and mould 9 inches in middle and 7 inches at the ends.
KNEES. To have two 6 inch Hackmatack Knees in each berth of Beams for fore and aft Knees, and 10 standing 8 inch Knees on each side of lower deck, to be of Hackmatack.
HATCH COAMINGS. To be 7 inches thick on upper deck, of White Oak.
PLANK. On bottom from Keel to Wales to be 3 inches thick of Yellow Pine where practicable. Fore and aft hoods to be of White Oak where thought necessary.
WALES. To have 9 streaks of Wales, upper streak to be 4 inches thick to increase to 4½ inches thick and diminish to the bottom planks.

The space between Wales and Plank Sheer to be planked with 3 inch plank about 5 inches wide, all to be of Yellow Pine when practicable.
CHAIN BOLTS. The Chain Bolts to be driven through the 4 inch streak below the Plank Sheer. Bolts to be 1½ inch iron for Fore and Main, 1¼ inch iron for Mizzen and all to be well riveted on the inside of the Vessel.
CHANNELS. To be about 5 inches wide and to be placed on the streak below the Plank Sheer, and not to cover any butts.
WATER WAY. To have a log Water Way 8 by 10 to 12 inches of Yellow Pine.
PLANK SHEER. To be 4 inches thick and wide enough to cover Water Way and outside planking with projection to be of Yellow Pine.
RAIL. To be 4½ inches thick and about 12 inches wide of Yellow Pine and to be fastened with galvanized iron.

BREAST HOOKS. To have 6 Breast Hooks and Pointers, two below the lower deck, one in the deck frame, one between decks, one in upper deck frame and one over the Bowsprit.

FASTENINGS. The floors to be fastened with 1 inch copper bolts to the Keel. The lower keelson to be fastened with 1⅛ inch copper bolts to be driven through each alternate floor timber and riveted on bottom of keel. Lower dead wood, Stem, Keel and Apron to be fastened with copper as high up as the vessel is to be metalled. Bottom planks to be fastened with composition spikes sufficient to work the plank snug to timbers and to be square fastened with locust treenails driven through and wedged on inside and outside.

Wales to be fastened with composition spikes sufficient to work them and fastened with locust treenails, to have three fastenings on each frame. The butts in bottom and Wales to be fastened with composition bolts 7 inches long and the butts in bottom plank to have a center treenail in the timbers each side of each butt.

Rider Keelson to be fastened with iron bolts of same size and in same manner as Mr. Samuel Damon fastens his Ship now building in New Bedford.

Deck frames to be thoroughly fastened in every particular with suitable sizes of iron never to be less size than those used by Mr. Damon, and all out and in bolts to be plugged on outside and riveted on the knees. Fastenings in outside Counter Timber of composition. Plank Sheer to be fastened through the Stanchions with copper bolts, other fastenings in Plank Sheer to be galvanized iron.

Bulwarks and Quick Work forward to be fastened with composition bolts or spikes and plugged. Planking on Stern outside and in fastened with composition or galvanized iron and bunged.

Lower deck to be fastened with galvanized iron. Upper deck to be fastened with galvanized iron and bunged.

All other fastenings, for any and all parts of the Ship not enumerated above, are to be of such size as is being used in the Construction of the Ship now building in New Bedford.

MONKEY RAIL. To have a Monkey Rail about 14 inches high from main rail to go from forward part of main rigging to Hurricane House bulwark boards, same to be fastened with composition. Also Monkey Rail of same height in wake of fore rigging, but without bulwark boards.

CABIN. To be finished with Pine according to Plans to be furnished by the Party of the Second Part, and painted, grained or varnished as the said Party may decide, with Steerage and Forecastle finished the usual manner of whaling vessels built in New Bedford.

SKYLIGHT. And Gang Ways to be put in and finished according to plan furnished by Party of Second Part. Skylight to be fastened with copper or composition.

RUDDER. To furnish and make a Rudder as directed by Party of Second Part.

BITTS & CLEATS. Bowsprit bitts to be 10 by 15 inches, of Yellow Pine. Bowsprit bed to be of first quality White Pine 24 inches wide and 4½ inches thick.

To furnish all bitts necessary for belaying and Whaling purposes. To be of White Oak where required. To have two Locust topsail sheet bitts to main mast, finished in like manner as Ship James Arnold. Windlass bitts to be of White Oak.

STANCHIONS. In lower hold to be 8 inches square of Oak, with cap to beams and tennant in Keelson. Upper deck Stanchions to be of Yellow Pine 6 inches square cleated top and bottom or with caps.

STANCHIONS. On deck to be of first quality Locust to side from 7 to 8 inches, and of same length as those now being put into Ship building in New Bedford. To be painted or Varnished as may be decided by the Party of the Second Part.

WINDLASS. To furnish a 24 inch Oak Windlass with Iron necks and boxes of suitable size. Haselton's 24 inch Ex Heavy Windlass Gear and to put on in suitable manner, such Iron whelps as the Party of the Second Part may furnish, and cut such Handspike holes as may be required. To be 9 feet between bitts. Heads 18 inches long.

IRON WORK. To furnish Chain Plates for fore and main mast of 1¼ inch round iron. Fore and main top mast back stays of same size with lignumvitae dead eyes of suitable dimensions, the rest of chain plates to be of suitable size, with dead eyes or bull eyes as may be thought best. No preventer bolts. To furnish all the ring bolts, eye bolts etc. which will be necessary for the deck, waist, side and bow, the same to be put in and fastened in a satisfactory manner. To furnish all Iron work for bowsprit and Jib Boom. The Hatch Coamings on upper deck. For Fore and Main are to be Ironed with flat Iron of suitable thickness and width, properly made and fastened, the Iron plates and fastenings to be galvanized.

HAWSE PIPES. To furnish and put in 2 Hawse Pipes, also 2 pipes on starboard side and one on port side forward, all to be well leaded with heavy lead.

CAULKING. To caulk the outside and decks of the vessel with the best of new Oakum, to be done in a thorough and satisfactory manner.

SALT STOPS. To put in 3 sets of Salt Stops where required.

GALLEY. To furnish a cooking Galley as per plan and size furnished by Party of the Second Part.

CARVED WORK. To furnish Billet Heads. Trail Boards.

PUMPS. To furnish White Pine Pumps, (2) of sufficient size, to be well banded with Iron, to have Cast Iron Chambers, with Iron Standards on deck, the finish of the whole to be like Ship James Arnold.

STEERING WHEEL. To furnish a travelling steering Wheel of Mahogany with Locust tiller and standards. Copper bolt through barrel and composition boxes in standards.

PAINT. To furnish and put on two good coats of paint outside the vessel from Copper line.

Seams above Copper to have four coats of paint. Seams in bottom to be payed with tar and rosin. Bottom to have a good coat of tar and rosin as far up as the Copper line.

WATER CLOSET. To furnish a Water Closet with Wash Bowl and Fixtures in Cabin, with lead tank and suitable connections for filling the same and let off for Bowl. Also to finish in house aft, a Water Closet without Bowl, but with lead pipe going down through the Ship in same manner as Ship James Arnold.

SPARS. To furnish a set of Spars of such sizes and lengths as per plan to be furnished by the Party of the Second Part. The Bowsprit and the lower masts to be set. Bowsprit bed to be Coppered and the masts to be properly wedged, all spars to have one coat of paint.

To furnish all necessary wooden and Iron cleats, chocks and cavils that may be required for the vessel's hull, also 6 Iron chocks forward to go on top of wooden chocks. To have a suitable lash rail properly fastened with galvanized Iron to Stanchions, by bolts which are to be ruffed upon the outside before the bulwarks are put on.

HURRICANE HOUSE. To build a hurricane house with Companion Ways and Water Closet room on the one side, and room or rooms on the other, as the Party of the Second Part may desire, the whole to be similar to Ship James Arnold.

UPPER DECK PLANK. To be of first quality White Pine 3 by 6 inches and to have two coats of varnish.

SALT. To be furnished by the Party of the Second Part and put in by the builders.

The top of deck beams, carlins and knees to be well varnished before the upper deck is laid, also ceiling etc. between decks.

The composition rudder braces, composition plates on stem, Side Lights, Stem Lights, and compositions for Gang Way and Skylight Guards are to be furnished by the Party of the Second Part but put on by the builders.

The work on the vessel to be done in a good substantial, workmanlike manner, and all the materials to be of good merchantable quality, and the vessel, when complete, according to this agreement—to be equal to—in all respects, and to compare favorably with the Ship now building in New Bedford by Samuel Damon.

The Boat Gear complete to be furnished and put up by the Party of the Second Part.

Yellow Pine shoeing on keel to be furnished and put on by Party of the First Part.

The vessel to be finished according to this agreement and delivered afloat in Port Jefferson harbor, as a tight ship, as near the first of May as may be found practicable by the builders.

The said vessel to be considered the property of the said Party of the Second Part, in every stage of her construction, as fast as paid for.

For and in consideration of the above named agreement, the said Party of the Second Part agrees to pay the Party of the First Part the sum of Fifteen Thousand Dollars, ($15,000) to be paid as follows:

One fifth of the amount when the keel is laid. One fifth when the frame is raised and regulated. One fifth when ceiled out and wales are on. One fifth when planked up and upper deck frame is in, and the balance when launched, and this contract is complete.

In witness whereof we the parties have hereunto set our hands day and date above written.

SIGNED

James M. Bayles & Son

SIGNED

Taber, Gordon & Co.